A CURE

for the

GROWLY BUGS

and Other Tried-and-True
Tips for Moms

A CURE

for the

GROWLY BUGS

and Other Tried-and-True Tips for Moms

From mothers of MOPS
Compiled by **MARY BETH LAGERBORG**

ZondervanPublishingHouse
Grand Rapids, Michigan

A Division of HarperCollins*Publishers*

MOTHERS OF
M♥PS
PRESCHOOLERS

A Cure for the Growly Bugs and Other Tried-and-True Tips for Moms
Copyright © 1997 by MOPS International, Inc.

Requests for information should be addressed to:

📖 ZondervanPublishingHouse
Grand Rapids, Michigan 49530

Library of Congress Cataloging-in-Publication Data

A cure for the growly bugs and other tried-and-true tips for moms: from mothers of MOPS / compiled by Mary Beth Lagerborg.
    p. cm.
    ISBN: 0-310-21135-2 (pbk.)
    1. Preschool children. 2. Child rearing. I. Lagerborg, Mary Beth.
HQ774.5.C87 1997
649'.123-dc 21   97-10361
                                                  CIP

Published in association with the literary agency of Alive Communications, 1465 Kelly Johnson Blvd., Suite 320, Colorado Springs, CO 80920.

Interior design by Sue Vandenberg Koppenol

Printed in the United States of America

97 98 99 00 01 02 03 04 /❖ DH/ 10 9 8 7 6 5 4 3 2 1

CONTENTS

ACKNOWLEDGMENTS

A Cure for the Growly Bugs and Other Tried-and-True Tips for Moms was a true team effort, with hundreds of women contributing their tips to provide down-to-earth advice for their sister moms. Thanks to all the women who gave their tips. You're terrific!

Thanks to Cindy Sumner, editor of MOPS' *MomSense* newsletter, for her wealth of good tips for moms, cheerfully given.

Thanks to Dave and Claudia Arp, who have made available to MOPS their wealth of wisdom for moms.

Thanks to Carol Kuykendall and Brenda Quinn at MOPS International, who lent their ears, sharp eyes, and passion for excellence.

Thanks to our team at Zondervan Publishing House, especially Sandy Vander Zicht and Rachel Boers, for their hearts as well as their expertise.

Thanks to Rick Christian, president of Alive Communications, for his patience and steady advocacy.

And finally, thanks to my husband, Alex, and sons Tim, Dan, and Andrew Lagerborg. You are such a joy that I want to be the best mom I can be.

INTRODUCTION

Kim padded in her slippers and bathrobe to Jacob's bedroom. He stood in the crib, holding onto the headboard and bouncing up and down on the mattress as if it were a trampoline. When he saw her, he stopped and shrieked gleefully, his shock of dark hair standing out at odd angles, his cheeks rubbed bright pink by the sheets, his brown eyes sparkling in anticipation of the day's adventures. Looking at him, Kim wanted to both scoop him into her arms and flee back to the kitchen and her coffee mug.

A packed day loomed ahead: caring for Jacob and his older sister, the preschool's field trip to a local farm, and three hours at her part-time bookkeeping job. But, she admitted, she enjoyed these tasks. It was all the other stuff—the endless circle of meals, the piles of laundry that grew like yeast, the errands with children in tow, and those stacks of bills and papers. Each day it was a battle to control these "giants" and concentrate on the really important stuff. The family stuff. The enjoy-those-children-because-they-grow-up-so-fast stuff. She longed for a refrigerator door with three dispensers: ice, water, and friendly advice about how to make her life easier.

This book is a collection of such advice, tips, and tid-bits for you from moms involved in MOPS (Mothers of Preschoolers), who meet to encourage and learn from one another. It is our hope that their voices will come through this book to you as if from the kitchen table over coffee, from across the back fence, or from the playground at the neighborhood park.

With their help, may you conquer the "giants" in your life and get to the good stuff.

ON THE ROAD
OR IN THE SKY

Diane glanced into the rearview mirror. She counted six little boy heads—three sons and three friends— in the minivan seats behind her. "Does everyone have his seat belt on?" she asked, maneuvering through traffic. It was Tuesday, and they were going to the beach at a nearby reservoir. She had blocked off the afternoon and had left early enough to beat the late-afternoon crowds. Stowed behind the backseat were sandwiches, chips, lemonade, water, beach balls, plastic tubs, beach towels, and sunscreen. She met her own gaze in the mirror and grinned. For once, she felt organized and prepared.

"Ryan doesn't," a voice came from the back.

"Ryan, buckle your seat belt," she said firmly but cheerfully.

"I don't want to."

"We all have our seat belts on, and you need yours on too." She glared at him through the rearview mirror.

Ryan was a rowdy one. She wanted that seat belt on him, low and tight.

"I don't have to."

Diane changed to the far right lane, glanced at the traffic behind her, slowed the van, and pulled onto the shoulder, tires screeching for effect. Shifting the van into park, she turned around in her seat to face six sober little faces, eyes riveted upon her. "In my car you do have to, Ryan, so I guess we'll all just wait here until you do." All eyes turned to Ryan.

"Come on, Ryan. Hurry up!" one whispered.

"Yeah, come on, Ryan. You gotta wear your seat belt."

Diane watched. Finally, slowly, with the quietest little "click," Ryan buckled up. But as Diane watched, she thought she caught something in his eyes, in his set lips. This four-year-old didn't take defeat lightly. She had scored the first victory, but what challenges would she face with this child during the hours ahead?

Establish a way station close to the door, yet out of sight to entering guests, to speed everyone out the door in the morning. Teach children to hang their coats and to pile backpacks, signed permission slips, items to mail, shoes or boots, lunch money, and completed homework here.

Talk with your children before you take them shopping or on an outing about where you're going, how long it will take, what behavior you expect, and any reward that will come for good behavior.

Give a warning to your child who is a dawdler: "In ten minutes we are leaving for preschool" or "Five minutes until bath time."

Avoid going anywhere when you or the children are tired.

Give each child her own small backpack or fanny pack with snacks and tissues for outings. Invest in a backpack for yourself!

Keep a small cooler in the back of the car packed with snacks: apples or fig bars, grapes, thin pretzel sticks, caramel rice cakes, graham crackers, sesame bread sticks, string cheese, miniboxes of raisins, oyster crackers, animal crackers, yogurt cups, or melon balls.

Engrave on a dog tag the name of the stuffed animal your child totes everywhere. Include the child's name and your telephone number, and affix the tag to the animal's tail or another suitable spot.

Dress yourself and your child in layers when traveling by air. Temperatures can fluctuate on a long flight, and the climate may be far different at your destination than at your point of departure.

Choose an object such as a church, a tractor, or a decorated mailbox for each child to look for when

13

traveling by car. Each child must find as many of his object as he is years old. Whoever finds his number first is the winner.

— — — — — — —

Plan a new activity for each hour of driving to keep children mentally occupied against the constant "how long till we get there?" At intervals, have them read aloud, play a game with one parent in the backseat, choose a toy from mom's bag, color quietly, listen to a story on tape, sing songs together, and eat snacks.

— — — — — — —

Stop for a ten-minute break for every two hours of driving. If possible, pack a picnic lunch instead of eating in a restaurant so that the children aren't going from one confining space to another.

— — — — — — —

Cut short crankiness or loudness in the car with this game: The first person to talk, giggle, or make a sound loses. The last to do so wins.

— — — — — —

Become everyone's favorite "car pool mom" by stowing individual juice containers and a simple snack in a cooler in the back of the car.

— — — — — — —

Pack an extra fingernail clipper in your car's glove compartment or in the diaper bag to trim the baby's fingernails and toenails while he or she sleeps in the car seat.

— — — — — — —

When camping, attach bells to a toddler's shoes or clothing so that you can hear her if she wanders away.

Take along bread crumbs to feed the ducks and the fish when you go camping or to a lake.

Stow a bag of gummy worms or other favorite treat in the car glove compartment when you go camping. If you end up waiting out a storm in the car, you will have a snack ready.

Designate the child who balks at fastening his seat belt as the official Navigator. Don't start the car until the Navigator assures you that all passengers are buckled up.

Maintain a "care kit" in the car. Consider including: extra diapers, wet wipes, plastic bags for dirty diaper disposal, a few "car only" toys, bandages, sunscreen, adult and children's acetaminophen (in a childproof container), an empty water bottle, an extra set of clothes for a young child, hats with visors, a blanket, old sweatshirts or jackets, an umbrella, snacks that won't spoil, an empty baby bottle or sippy cup with lid, audiotapes, and books. Pack all the items in a toolbox or a plastic storage box with a fitted lid.

Keep a plastic laundry basket in the trunk of the car for books, coats, and backpacks.

Sign up for AAA or another road service if you have young children and may find yourself on the side of the road needing help.

Teach children to stand next to the car on the yellow parking line or "safety spot" while you load and unload car seats and packages from the car.

Take your time and enjoy things as they happen. It doesn't do any good to try to hurry. Most of the time a child has his own schedule.

Read aloud when the whole family is riding in the car together for trips. Over time, you will be able to read whole series of books to this captive audience. Choose books appropriate to the average age of your children. Vary your reading with joke books, magazine articles, or seasonal poems.

Take family trips. Many of the best family memories come from these trips, so they are worth the trouble. The good trips provide a lifelong store of happy memories for a child; the bad trips at least become a shared adventure.

Pack each child's complete outfit for each day in separate zip-closure bags labeled with the child's name. The child can then pick a baggie for the day and dress himself.

Stop by your local library before leaving on a trip and check out some book/cassette tape combinations so kids can read along with the audio version of a story.

Take along a night light, a baby monitor, and a supply of large plastic trash bags when traveling with young children. The night light can help ease a child's fears when staying in a strange room, the baby monitor will allow you time to relax outdoors while your child naps, and the trash bags can go under a bed wetter's bottom sheet or can be used to hold dirty laundry.

Pack one or two bags with all necessary toiletries and a couple changes of clothes for each family member. Be sure this bag is the last one packed in the car, and it will be the only one you'll have to unload for an overnight stay.

Put some infant spoons in a toothbrush holder if you are traveling with an infant. They will stay clean and be easy to find.

Make frequent rest stops when traveling with children. Take a ball or jump rope or Frisbee to encourage a good stretch for all. Change places at each rest stop so that everyone gets to sit next to a different person and has a different view from the car.

Type a card to put in each child's pocket giving his name, parents' names, and the phone number of your home or the hotel where you are staying for a trip. Dress the whole family in a similar color for ease in finding each other if separated in a crowd, and let the children wear whistles around their necks to blow if they get lost.

Lend your child something you use frequently— a hat or nightshirt or mug—when you are traveling and your child stays home.

Take along an umbrella stroller when flying with children. That way you can push the child all the way to his seat, then stow the stroller in the overhead bin.

Use a fanny pack instead of a purse on an airplane. A purse can fall off your shoulder as you bend and lift. With a fanny pack, you'll have one less bag to carry, and your money and tickets are right with you.

Hold a small infant in a front carrier on an airplane so the child feels secure and your hands are free. Be sure the seat belt is around you, not around the baby carrier.

Nurse a baby or give her a bottle or pacifier on takeoffs and landings. Take along gum for older children to chew.

Ask, when making airplane reservations, to be seated in a row with a vacant seat between you (if both parents are flying), or next to you (if one parent).

Pack a novel toy or game for a child to open on a trip. Choose one with few pieces, so you don't have to worry about losing the parts.

Bring a child's pail full of water to the car as you leave the beach. Have each child dunk his feet in it to wash off the sand before stepping into the car.

Store beach toys in a plastic laundry basket or mesh bag. Before leaving the beach for the day, dunk the basket or bag to rinse the toys of sand.

IN THE KITCHEN

I know, Mommy—let's bake bread!" Seven-year-old J.R. loved to help Michele cook. She enjoyed it too, if she felt rested and didn't have her three-year-old daughter, Jacque, underfoot, and if she could control what they were making and contain the mess.

But on this morning even Michele felt playful. It was as though her perfectionist button had flipped to "off." She felt almost giddy, as if she were being naughty.

"Okay, J.R.," she replied.

He looked at her quizzically, noting the dance in her dark eyes. "How do you bake bread, Mom?"

"I don't know. But I bet we can figure it out."

Without consulting a cookbook, they hauled out a big mixing bowl and the ingredients they decided they would need: flour, sugar, eggs, and shortening. Michele stood Jacque on a chair and wrapped a big apron around her. They all mixed, punched, and kneaded, adding fistfuls of flour. Soon a white film covered the counter, the floor, and filled every crevice in the kitchen.

Before long, the aroma of fresh bread wafted through the kitchen, and even the cleaning up seemed fun, caught as they were in wonder at the all-pervasiveness of the flour around them.

Then out of the oven it came. The loaf was really bread! A little flat perhaps, but when they tested it out at dinner, even Dad said it didn't taste too bad. The whole experience left Michele wondering why she hadn't let the kids have this kind of fun in the kitchen more often.

Plan menus for the week to cut down on waste and trips to the supermarket. As often as possible, make double batches and freeze one batch for a particularly hectic day.

Clip coupons, or circle the ones you want and have your child cut them out. Try to shop where you can get double coupon value, and use coupons on sale items to get the absolute lowest price. Share some of the money saved with the child who clipped the coupons.

Write your grocery list on the front of an envelope, then keep coupons you will need for these products in the envelope.

Keep track, using a small notebook, of the prices of items you buy regularly, so you can determine which of your local stores really does offer the best prices.

List on a sheet of paper the general contents of each aisle in your grocery store, creating a column for each aisle. Make several copies of this sheet and use it to record your shopping list by aisles.

Choose and read the recipes for what you will prepare for dinner either that day by 9:00 A.M. or the night before. This eliminates surprises such as "marinate meat for one hour," which can throw meal preparation off balance.

Keep a child-size apron in the kitchen. When you are there to watch, pull up a sturdy kitchen chair, put the back of the chair against the counter, and let your child stand to measure ingredients or stir.

Store a basket or bucket filled with small plastic containers, ladles, and strainers under the sink. Let your child play with some water and these items at the sink while you cook. Add soap for bubble fun. Older preschoolers can help out by washing vegetables and unbreakable cookware.

Remove the odor of chopped onion or garlic from a wood chopping block by sprinkling the wood surface with baking soda and rubbing it with a damp sponge or cloth.

Keep breakfast from becoming ho-hum for you and your family. Instead of cereal, serve a big bowl of popcorn (for preschoolers or older children who manage popcorn without choking), toasted peanut butter sandwiches, or parfaits of layered yogurt, fruit, and granola.

Make ice-cream sandwiches by spreading softened ice cream or frozen yogurt on an Oreo or a graham cracker square and gently placing an identical cookie on top.

Create sandwiches in fun shapes or with faces by pressing cookie cutters through them. Let your child choose the shapes and cut the sandwiches.

Wash fresh vegetables as soon as you get home from the store. Slice them and keep them in zip-closure bags in the refrigerator where the family will see them and think to eat them more often.

Avoid cooking during the hour before dinner if it's your family's worst time of the day. Instead, use entrees you've frozen or make meals in the morning, when your energy level is higher.

Take out a favorite game, book, or toy for your child while you prepare dinner, or—better yet—have the child help stir or crack eggs or take things out of the cupboards or refrigerator.

Follow these grocery shopping tips:

- Post an ongoing shopping list on the refrigerator, jotting down items as you need them. If a family member needs shampoo, ask that person to write it on the list.
- Plan menus for the week, adding needed ingredients to your running grocery list.
- Shop only once a week, alone if possible, to save money and time.
- Study supermarket specials.
- Use a calculator as you shop to avoid a big surprise at the checkout counter.
- Pay with cash if you are trying to keep your expenditures on groceries within strict limits.

Freeze leftover cooked vegetables, meat, and noodles in a container for soup. When the container is full, thaw it and add canned tomato soup, beef or chicken broth, and spices—use your imagination. It's an inexpensive meal and never the same soup twice.

Remove wax from candleholders by leaving the candleholders in the freezer for a few hours. The wax will then peel off easily.

Buy an apron you like and wear it to protect your clothing from stains when you're cooking or feeding the baby.

— — — — — — —

Try a cooking co-op if you have two neighbors who would be willing. Three times a week only one family cooks, tripling the menu and delivering the extra servings to the other two families. Meet once a month to discuss new menu ideas and schedule changes.

— — — — — — —

Sit down together as a family, at a set table, for at least one meal a day.

— — — — — — —

Teach proper table manners at the family table. At the same time you will be teaching respect, kindness, and politeness. Concentrate on one point at a time, such as passing salt and pepper to your right ("Right is always right."). Make it a game. See if you can catch one another doing it correctly. A good resource for teaching etiquette to children is *The Family Book of Manners* by Hermine Hartley.

— — — — — — —

Light a candle when the family gathers for dinner. Have each person share the best thing that happened to each of them that day.

— — — — — — —

Take advantage of seasonal berries such as fresh strawberries, blueberries, and raspberries, by rinsing them well, draining them in a colander, and freezing them on cookie sheets. When they are frozen, package them in zip-closure bags and enjoy them later from the freezer.

Use terry cloth towels for napkins and bibs.

Never put more milk in a cup than you are willing to clean up.

Put a small portion of each food on a child's plate. Teach her to take two "no thank you" bites without complaining if she does not like a particular food, then leave the rest if she wishes.

Give a child a drinking straw. Besides being fun to use, it helps develop the small muscles in the lips that are needed for forming certain sounds—that of "w," for example.

Serve cereal or soup in a cup or mug with a handle, so that the child can easily drink the milk or remaining broth.

Fill the compartments of a muffin tin with different finger foods, such as cheese cubes, strips of cold meat, crackers, raw vegetables, and fruit for a potpourri lunch.

Serve a meal on a doll plate, an aluminum pie plate, or a new (washed) Frisbee just for fun.

Mix yogurt or applesauce, instead of milk, with cereal for a manageable solid when a child is mastering handling the spoon.

Fill an ice-cream cone with tuna or egg salad, cottage cheese, or yogurt for an easy, fun lunch.

Give each child a small water jug of his own to keep in the refrigerator.

Use an ice-cream scoop to fill the paper baking cups when making cupcakes. The batter will pour into the cups neatly and the cupcakes will be a uniform size.

Avoid getting chocolate cake crumbs in white icing! Apply a thin layer of white icing to a chocolate cake, then refrigerate the cake for fifteen to twenty minutes. The thin layer of icing will harden, trapping the crumbs. Finish frosting the cake with the remaining icing.

Visit a farmer's market with your child and buy fresh fruits and vegetables for snack time. Visit a farm to harvest a favorite food, like apples, peaches, or strawberries.

Invest in a vinyl tablecloth with a flannel backing for picnics in the park, casual dining indoors, and for messy projects like pumpkin carving. Wipe it down with a damp cloth after use, and store it after it's thoroughly dry.

Go to the food court at a mall when shopping with small children. Each child can order from a different restaurant. For a learning game, see who can find the best food value for the same amount of money. An added benefit: You can get your food quickly, and if a baby cries, you can push him in the stroller.

Designate one person to help you in the kitchen and another to watch the children when you have company for a big meal or on holidays.

Make an overnight guest feel cozy and welcome with the following guest-room supplies: a pot of hot water, mugs, and a small basket of packages of instant hot chocolate, apple cider, tea, and coffee. (Don't forget packets of sugar and nondairy creamer!) In another basket, provide fresh fruits and healthful snacks.

MAKING MEMORIES

Becky tilted her head back and rocked slowly. Outside the window the rain continued. The sky sagged low and gray, but the drenched leaves were a vivid, dark green. Nestled against her neck was a warm, soft fuzzy head. Ericka's little back was bowed out in her soft nightie, curling her in a cozy ball.

Becky's thoughts slipped to the upholstered rocker beneath her. It was a simple piece of furniture, like a lazy "L" with a flourish at the top where it curved behind her neck. When she rocked Ericka, she liked to remember that this rocker had been her great-great-grandmother's. How many women in her family had rocked their babies in this chair?

She felt a connectedness, a strength borrowed from these women she had never known, yet who seemed a part of her and of Ericka. They too had held in their arms babies for whom they had prayed and dedicated their lives to raising. She hoped that someday she could pass on this same heritage to the daughter in her arms.

Buy a special pen at a camera store and save it for writing on the backs of your photographs. With it, date and identify the people in all your photographs, even if you don't write an elaborate caption.

Kneel or squat at the child's level and get as close as you can when photographing children. Eliminate unnecessary elements in the picture. For a posed shot, give children something to play with. Take your shot on the count of two instead of three. For more candid shots, "finish" your photo session but start shooting again when your subjects relax.

Take disposable cameras on outings. Give one to each child and let them snap away!

Mix an occasional roll of black-and-white film with your color shots. Black-and-white pictures last longer than those taken with color film, and they offer their own distinctive look. Be aware, however, that they may be more expensive to develop—and they may take longer.

Show that your family is important. On desks, dressers, mantels, tables, a piano—all around your home—keep framed pictures of ancestors and family members. Keep in your purse a list of the sizes of photos for which you need frames and watch for them to come on sale.

Establish mealtime as a memorable time when you tune in to one another. Turn off the TV and eat together in the dining room or on a deck or porch. If you have young children, gear the conversation to an appropriate length of time for them to sit still and eat. Then either hold a young child on a lap or excuse him from the table and let the older children and parents linger and talk.

Videotape a family gathering. Prepare questions ahead of time for each family member to answer, drawing out stories from the oldest grandma to the youngest (talking) child.

Make a scrapbook of what was happening on the day your child was born or adopted. On each page glue newspaper clippings showing that day's clothing styles, popular books and music, weather, headlines, and sports events. Record your feelings about your new baby and your hopes for his life.

Keep a journal for your child. Start while you are pregnant or anticipating adoption and write entries periodically throughout her childhood and youth. Keep track of different stages, things she says or likes to do, elements of her personality.

Show your child a picture of yourself as a child. Show him pictures of where you lived and played.

Talk about your pets. Tell stories about your grand-parents and where they lived.

— — — — — — —

Create a family time capsule with photos, a newspaper's front page, a few favorite outgrown toys, audio- and videotapes of special family gatherings, a music CD, a favorite team's logo—use your imagination.

— — — — — — —

Write a letter to your child each year on his birthday, telling what you love about him, his hobbies, interests, accomplishments, continual questions, anything that may have been meaningful to him and to you over the past year. Tell how proud you are of him and how much God loves him. Include this in your child's journal.

— — — — — — —

Document in your journal—with samples—the evolution of your child's handwriting. In addition, record her feelings, thoughts, and events in her life.

— — — — — — —

If you are too busy to write cute things in your child's baby book or journal as they happen, tape-record observations you can later write in the book. The tapes can make a great keepsake too!

— — — — — — —

Collect Christmas stories and keep them in a basket. Let your child choose a book from the basket to read each night in December.

— — — — — — —

Stop what you are doing for five minutes at some point in the day and just watch your child, snapping memories from the invisible Polaroid in your heart. Remember that even the most exhausting days have golden moments to treasure; little ones grow up so fast.

Document the very special event of the adoption of a child, including a scrapbook of photos and congratulatory letters from family and friends. Ask a friend to videotape the parents receiving the news, preparing the nursery, talking about the upcoming event, and receiving the child.

Show your child videos or photos you took of her as a newborn to prepare her for the arrival of a baby brother or sister. These will show her what a newborn really looks like, as well as how much she was loved as a baby. This can spark some wonderful, warm times of reminiscing with your child, and help her know how special she is as she anticipates a sibling.

Videotape special events in a story format with a beginning, middle, and end. Cut away occasionally from the main activity to capture other's actions and reactions. Make sure to hold the camera still to avoid giving later viewers a seasick feeling.

Mat or frame a selection of your child's artistic masterpieces for your office wall or a basement recreation room.

— — — — — — —

Store your child's masterpieces flat and avoid bending or folding them whenever possible. If you hang artwork on a wall or refrigerator, keep it out of direct sunlight. Never mount artwork with glue or rubber cement.

— — — — — — —

If you don't have the room or the inclination to store all your child's creations, periodically sit your child on the floor and take a picture of him surrounded by a selection of his recent arts and crafts.

— — — — — — —

Buy a beautiful plate of a pattern different than your regular dinnerware and use this "special plate" to honor a family member on a special occasion (such as a birthday) or for an accomplishment. Remember to recognize as well such "accomplishments" as generosity and helpfulness.

— — — — — — —

Hang a favorite baby photo of the birthday child on the front door to welcome birthday guests.

— — — — — — —

Decorate with colorful beach balls instead of balloons if infants and small children will attend a birthday celebration. Balloons can pose a choking hazard to small children.

— — — — — — —

Take pictures of your birthday party decorations and refreshments before the party, not just during or after the party.

— — — — — — —

Prescoop ice cream into short, wide, clear plastic tumblers before the birthday party. Add a spoon. Place cups on a tray and freeze them. At cake time, just pull them out of the freezer and hand them out. There's no more sliding or melting ice cream on the cake plate, and children can dig in easily.

— — — — — — —

Slip in the treat bag of each guest a Polaroid photo of the birthday child with the guest and his gift. Write, "Thank you. I'm glad you came!" on the back, from the birthday child.

— — — — — — —

Show your child pictures of her parents and older siblings when they were her age.

— — — — — — —

Celebrate the first fire of the season by gathering around the fireplace with popcorn and apple cider or hot chocolate.

— — — — — — —

Invite everyone to write his blessings in a remembrance book on Thanksgiving Day. Younger children will enjoy dictating their thankfulness. Each Thanksgiving, read the lists from previous years. Children will enjoy recalling what they were thankful for in past years.

— — — — — — —

Make a long family walk mandatory on Thanksgiving. Take a walk before you eat and savor the smells as you walk back into the house. (Or stagger out afterward before you explode!)

Stock up on stamps, film, batteries, tape, paper plates, cups, and napkins in November so you have them on hand—and can avoid the expense of them— in December.

Hire teenage baby-sitters you may need in December during November, before they commit to someone else. Since you're scheduling so far ahead, call a week before the date to confirm. Ask the sitter to arrive thirty minutes before your departure so you can have some time to yourself to get ready.

Hire a baby-sitter to entertain your children if you are having a party in your home. Ask the sitter to come early to entertain the children while you prepare.

Make a cut paper garland of twenty-four Christmas trees or gingerbread men cut from paper as an alternative to an advent calendar. Ask your children to contribute twenty-four ideas for easy family activities to write on the backs of cutout shapes. Cut one piece off the garland each night, and do the activity together.

Look for holiday craft ideas early. Go to the library and look for November and December issues of magazines from the previous year.

———————

Hide each piece of the nativity set somewhere in your living room before telling the Christmas story. Let your children hunt for the pieces. When they are all found, tell the Christmas story, letting each child contribute a nativity character when appropriate. Then leave the nativity set out so the children can retell the story themselves.

———————

Invest in shared experiences rather than in toys.

———————

After reading the Christmas story to your child a few times, ask your child to tell the story to you and tape-record it. Give the tape as a gift to family members and save it to replay in future years.

———————

Invite some other families or friends to join you caroling in your neighborhood. Take along bells for children to ring and flashlights to light your way. When you get home, enjoy Christmas treats such as hot chocolate and Christmas cookies.

———————

Enjoy a few family meals illuminated only by the Christmas tree.

———————

Drive around town viewing the Christmas lights with an elderly neighbor or friend.

Help an elderly neighbor or friend decorate her home for Christmas, and help put away her decorations at the end of the season.

———————

Select old Christmas cards with biblical Christmas scenes and symbols and use them as visual aids to teach your children the Christmas story.

———————

Decorate a pair of baby booties or socks for a memorable "First Christmas" ornament. Use fabric paint to write the child's name and the year, stuff with cotton, and attach a loop for hanging them on your tree.

———————

Plan rest periods along with activities and outings for your houseguests. Older visitors as well as small children will benefit from a break in the schedule.

BUILDING CHARACTER (SOMETIMES YOURS, SOMETIMES THEIRS)

A re you busy for the next couple of hours?"

Jan had just stationed her three-year-old in front of *Sesame Street* and begun to cook dinner when Peggy called, sounding discouraged.

"No . . . what's up?" Jan asked.

"Would you please come over and remove Toby from the house before I commit child abuse?"

Jan knew Peggy was kidding, yet there was a quiver in her friend's voice. Toby was a turbo of a two-year-old who kept Peggy weary.

"What happened?"

"Well, I was stirring chili on the stove when I heard the toilet flush upstairs."

"So?"

"So the only person upstairs was Toby, who was taking his nap."

"Uh oh."

"Yeah, well, the toilet sound didn't wrap up. It just kept running and running and running. Water began dripping through the light fixture into the breakfast room, so I ran upstairs to the bathroom.

"You know the little bathroom drawer where I keep my makeup? Well, he had pulled it out, added my watch and wedding ring from the counter for good measure, then dumped them all in the toilet, and flushed!"

"Oh, Peg," Jan said, feeling bad for her friend, "we'll be right over. I'll help you clean up the mess and then bring Toby back here to our house for dinner." Giving Peggy a break from Toby for a while would be the easy part. But how could she advise and encourage her friend?

Trust your instincts. You know your child best. Books and the advice of others may or may not prove helpful. Prayerfully weigh it all and then go with what seems right for your family. There is no one right way to parent.

Choose your battles carefully, but when you choose one, see it through to the conclusion. Don't engage in battles you can't win.

Think of the goal of discipline as teaching—not punishment. Children have to learn desired behavior.

Set boundaries for things that are important and let the rest go. Choose carefully the rules you establish, such as no back talking, being respectful to elders, and always letting a parent know where the child is going. Beyond these, if something is not unsafe, unhealthy, or immoral, try to say yes more than no. So what if your child wears unmatched clothes at home sometimes, or gets really messy or muddy, or eats something out of the ordinary for breakfast? For help in this area read *Getting Out of Your Kids' Faces and Into Their Hearts* by Valerie Bell.

Strive for consistency in your parenting, so children know what is expected of them. If you have answered, "No, we won't be able to go to the zoo today," teach your child there's no sense his asking that question again today.

Control carefully how much freedom and responsibility you give your children as they grow up. Some have compared freedom to a ball of string that can be let out but not withdrawn. If you give out too much too fast, you will have nothing left to allow them to do as adolescents. They may then go to extremes, pushing for even more privileges.

Never punish a child for childish (as opposed to defiant) behavior. Discipline disobedience and take the time to explain inappropriate childish behavior.

Respect the fragile self-esteem of a child and never ridicule or devalue a child for crying, for being afraid, or for wetting the bed.

Call in reinforcements to squeeze out the growly bugs or banish the blues. When a family member is cranky or sad, yell "Group hug!" and circle the family around the needy one for a family hug.

Take the stress out of bedtime. Decide at what time the bedtime routine must conclude with lights out and the last kiss and drink of water. Then calculate the amount of time it takes for putting on pajamas, brushing teeth, reading stories, and snuggles and prayers in order to decipher at what time you need to begin the process.

Keep rules simple. Ask yourself, "Is this a character flaw or someone just being a character?"

When a child is crying, stop and think HALT. Is this child: Hungry, Angry, Lonely, or Tired?

Keep things in perspective. Ask yourself, when a crisis or problem arises, "Will anyone care about this in ten years?"

Don't make your child live with a label you, or others, affix to her, such as "difficult," "strong-willed," or "immature."

Try to have your children follow the same rules while visiting as they do at home.

Squeeze out the growly bugs. When your child is grouchy, tell her you must hug her tightly to squeeze out the growly bugs. Then pretend to stomp out the escaping growly bugs.

Admit your mistakes and ask for your child's forgiveness. Let your child know that you are not perfect either. One mom says that when she gets on her boys too much, her oldest reminds her "I'm a gift from God, Mommy." This calms her and restores focus. Ask your children to remind you that they're gifts from God. It makes them feel good too!

Establish some ground rules when you have neighborhood children over. When playing at your house, a guest should follow the same rules as your child does—including helping pick up toys.

Use positive reinforcement to encourage behaviors you want to see in your children. For example, if you want a child to pick up his room, say something like, "I know you can do a wonderful job of picking up your room, and I'll bet you can do it as fast as you did last time. I was so proud of the obedient and cheerful way you cleaned up yesterday. I'll look forward to seeing how great you're going to do today." Then check to keep him on track, and praise and hug him when the job is finished.

— — — — — — —

Use these alternative methods to lashing out in anger:

- Take a deep breath. And another. Remember, you are the adult.
- Leave the room for a minute. Consciously breathe in and out. Whisper a prayer for perseverance and patience.
- Close your eyes and imagine you're hearing what your child is about to hear.
- Press your lips together and count to ten. Better yet, count to twenty.
- Put your child in a time-out chair (one time-out minute for each year of age).
- Put yourself in a time-out chair. Think about why you are angry. Is it your child's fault, or is your child simply a convenient target for your anger?
- Phone a friend.
- Go outside and take a walk (if someone can watch the children).
- Take a hot bath or splash cold water on your face.
- Hug a pillow.
- Turn on soothing music. Sing along.
- Pick up a pencil and write down things for which you are thankful. Keep the list.
- Put your baby in the crib, swing, or playpen when you've reached your limit.

— — — — — — —

Use humor when you need to tell your children something important. One mother gets down to her children's level, puts her fingers on their temples, and then makes a buzzing sound like brain waves going back and forth between their heads and hers. They look at her and smile, and then she has their attention. She also sometimes tells them she's Scar from the *Lion King* and they're the hyenas. In a harsh, Scar-like voice, she says, "Pay attention!" They think it's funny, and she gets their attention.

Apologize and ask your child to repeat what they were saying when you find yourself saying "Uh-huh" without really hearing him. It's amazing what new insights you can gain about your child just by listening.

Resist the need to be right just because you are the adult.

Whisper to get a child to listen. When you whisper into a child's ear, she will stop crying or yelling to hear what you're saying.

Listen to your child and don't act appalled or shocked at anything she tells you.

Tell your child that, "Out of all the children in the world, I'm so glad you are my child! I'll love you always!"

Catch your child doing something right and praise him for it.

———————

Stop and spend five minutes with your child when she becomes whiny and bothersome. When she acts this way, she needs you, not a toy or book. A child who is put off won't go away.

———————

Make that moment of separation when you leave your child in the care of someone else reassuring but quick. The longer you linger, the more confused your child will become as to whether or not you're really leaving. Give him a reassuring hug, tell him you'll be back soon, and let the caregiver take over.

———————

Keep close to the phone a few special toys which your children can play with quietly only while you're talking on the phone.

———————

Allow your child to use you as a scapegoat when he faces a scary situation. For example, if he is invited to another child's home and doesn't feel good about it, let him know it's okay to say, "My mother won't let me."

———————

Be patient. Ideas that work beautifully with one child may not fit another. Keep trying different ways to encourage and discipline each child.

———————

Don't argue with your spouse about the children in front of them.

Love your children. It is when they seem least lovable that they need your love the most.

Help your toddler pick up her toys by pretending that the two of you are "putting her toys to bed." This will help ease her to dreamland.

KEEPING HOUSE

It had rained all day today, and yesterday, and the day before yesterday, urging forth the tender April grass and making quagmires of the roadsides and construction sites.

Sandy pulled the minivan into the garage. She carefully freed sleeping four-year-old Josh from his seat belt, picked him up, lugged him into the house, and laid him on the sofa. Then, walking into the kitchen, she saw Cedric grinning at her through the sliding patio door.

"Cedric, you stupid dog!" Sandy pressed her forehead against the cool glass of the door and looked at him. The mutt panted cheerfully. Tail wagging, he was frosted with mud from muzzle to tail tip. Obviously he had dug under the fence again. But he was too dumb to run away; he always crawled back.

Sandy went to the garage, opened the side door, and called him. "You stay in here until I figure out what to do with you!" she commanded sternly, darting into the house again before Cedric could rub against her jeans.

Josh was sleeping soundly on the sofa, so Sandy took a basket of laundry upstairs and dumped it on her bed. Flipping on her favorite radio station, she began to fold T-shirts and match socks.

Suddenly she heard Josh squeal, "Ced-wick! You're a mess!" and before she could turn around, the dog bounded into her bedroom, shaking mud as he came. She tried to grab the slimy collar, but he lurched away again. Josh ran after Sandy who ran after Cedric down the stairs, through the family room, breakfast room, and kitchen, shaking dirty water on every piece of furniture, cabinet, wall, table, chair, and door. The chase ended back at the garage door, which Sandy opened and Cedric bounded through. She slammed it shut and turned to Josh, whose brow and chubby cheeks were contorted with remorse. "I'm sorry, Mommy!" he said.

Well sure, he was sorry, thought Sandy, as she gathered him up in a reassuring hug, *but how would she clean up this mess?*

— — — — — — —

Lower your standard of how often you need to thoroughly clean the house. Pick up clutter. Get paper-work organized and sort through mail daily. Take a hard look at unused household items and donate reusable things.

— — — — — — —

Clean up as much as possible as you go; then practice being satisfied that you have done your best. Keeping your house clean while you have small children is like shoveling while it's still snowing.

— — — — — — —

Leave an empty laundry basket in the front hall closet for a quick pick-up when the doorbell rings.

———————

Try to accomplish one major cleaning project each weekday—like vacuuming or cleaning the bathrooms—so that Saturday is not a marathon cleaning day.

———————

Do chores you don't like first (like cleaning the toilet).

———————

Invest in these handy items:
- A powerful vacuum cleaner.
- A dust buster.
- A dozen cloth diapers for dust rags.
- A sturdy apron with pockets in the front to wear while cleaning and gardening.
- A professional-quality squeegee from a janitorial supply store for washing windows.
- A quality cordless telephone.

———————

Hire a middle school student to help with baby-sitting, cleaning, and cooking.

———————

Try to keep one designated room of the house picked up and clean. It will provide a needed oasis for you, and a place where guests can sit.

———————

Use those fifteen-minute opportunities in every day to do a chore or two.

Pair two chores, like putting in a load of laundry and sweeping the porch, or cleaning off the kitchen counter while you make phone calls and appointments.

Let children help at small jobs while they are very young and think it's fun. Put into practice early, chores become second nature to children as they grow older. Do not pay children for basic household chores. (You are not paid for doing them either!) Teach your children that each family member's help is needed to keep the household running smoothly. When your child says "I do it," let him.

Involve your children in what you are doing so that they can learn the task while still allowing you to get the job done. For example, if you plant a vegetable garden, give them a small plot. Or give them dust-cloths while you dust. When doing paperwork, give them pencils or crayons and paper.

Have a family pick-up time just before bed. In the first room, ask the children to put into a laundry basket everything that doesn't belong in that room. Then have them put in their proper places the things that are left in the room. Move to the next room, removing from the basket things that belong in that room, and putting into the basket things that don't. This makes picking up less overwhelming. Waking up to an orderly home improves everyone's outlook on the day.

— — — — — — —

Teach children to put their shoes in a shoe bag on the back of a door and to hang their coats and hats on pegs mounted at their height.

— — — — — — —

Read, play, or snuggle when your child asks you to, if at all possible. It's so tempting to say, "Let's do it later" or "Mom's busy." But there will always be tasks to do, many of which can wait. A child's growing won't wait. Someday she won't want to play or read or even snuggle anymore.

— — — — — — —

Try this mixture for cleaning windows:

> 1/2 cup of ammonia
> 1 cup of white vinegar
> 1 tablespoon of cornstarch
>
> Combine in a bucket of warm water.

— — — — — — —

Give your house an inexpensive face-lift. With a friend or two to lend opinions, move the furniture and reposition pictures and knickknacks in your home.

— — — — — — —

Make this recipe for homemade baby wipes:

> 2 cups warm water
> 2–3 tablespoons baby bath or shampoo (brands you know are safe for your baby's skin)

1–2 tablespoons baby lotion or creamy oil
40–45 Bounty select-a-size paper towels, folded
    into thirds
An empty Baby Wipes container or comparable
    Tupperware container

Mix water, baby bath, and lotion. Pour 1/4 of the mixture over each addition of ten folded paper towels in the container. If wipes seem too wet, add more paper towels to the bottom of the container. If wipes are too dry, add a couple more tablespoons of the solution.

Not only are these wipes about three times less expensive than store brands, they are also great for babies who have particularly sensitive skin. Pack them on camping trips or picnics, and in diaper bags and car glove compartments.

— — — — — — —

Carry in your purse or diaper bag a small bottle of baking soda and water for when your baby throws up on you and you're away from home. Rub the spot with a cloth dampened in the mixture.

— — — — — — —

Remove stubborn food stains from clothes with a little bit of Suave shampoo.

— — — — — — —

Remove clothes promptly from the dryer. If you can't get to them, put a damp towel of similar color in with the wrinkled clothes and run the dryer for thirty minutes.

— — — — — — —

Corral Legos, doll clothes, crayons, markers, and puzzles in closet shoe bags, tackle boxes, zip-closure bags, clear plastic boxes, shoe boxes, or popcorn cans.

Store balls and sports equipment in plastic laundry baskets.

Keep a plastic bin of toys in your master bedroom closet or home office to enable children to entertain themselves while you are getting dressed or working at home.

Store bath toys in a plastic or rubber bin in the bathtub behind the shower curtain.

Reuse baby wipe containers to store baby's socks or T-shirts; toy cars; doll shoes and accessories; crayons, markers, and colored pencils; small sewing or craft items; cassette tapes; stamps and stamp pads; a first-aid kit for the car or office; or as a holder for all the treasures a child collects. Use them as dividers for a baby's or toddler's drawers, or to file recipe cards, bills, receipts, or photo negatives.

Reuse the plastic sleeves that hold newspapers by tucking them into the diaper bag for dirty diapers or wet clothes.

Put clothes away in sets when folding children's laundry. Pair together a shirt and matching pair of pants. Stuff a coordinating pair of socks in a sleeve.

— — — — — — —

Use comforters or quilts to keep bed-making easy.

— — — — — — —

Put toothbrushes in the silverware holder of the dishwasher and run them through with a load of dishes. This is great for when you find toothbrushes on the floor or in other not-so-clean places, or when you forget whose toothbrush is whose.

— — — — — — —

Clean your microwave by pouring two tablespoons of lemon juice in a microwaveable dish. Run the microwave on maximum power for two minutes. The sides easily wipe clean, and the kitchen smells good.

— — — — — — —

Use a color to identify each child's clothing if you have more than one child. Using a different color permanent marker for each child, draw a mark on the inside rim of socks and underpants. You can take this further and buy a toothbrush and a comb or hairbrush for each child in his or her color.

— — — — — — —

Use a skirt hanger with multiple tiers to organize mittens and hats.

— — — — — — —

Do one load of laundry a day to avoid a no-clean-clothes crisis.

— — — — — — —

Get a laundry basket for each person in the family and one for sheets and towels. Sort and fold clothes from the dryer into the individual laundry baskets. The children's laundry baskets can be delivery trucks that the children gas up and drive to their rooms to put away their clothes.

— — — — — — —

Clean slow-flowing drains by pouring 1/2 cup baking soda into the drain, followed by 1–2 cups of household (white) vinegar. Let this mixture bubble and foam for about ten minutes. Next, flush the drain with hot water for a minute or two, then flush it with cold water. This will not unstop a clogged drain, but should scour and freshen one that's slow-running.

— — — — — — —

Plan a shared work day with another family at each of their homes in the spring and fall. The shared chores go quickly and pleasantly. Finish the work day with a potluck supper.

— — — — — — —

Chase the no-money-to-spend blues by rearranging furniture and accessories, cleaning out closets, and maximizing what you do have.

— — — — — — —

Keep a few of your most-used tools in a kitchen or family room drawer. Include a hammer, a regular and a Phillips screwdriver, a measuring tape, and nails for hanging pictures.

Clean combs and brushes by tossing them in the laundry with a load of wash.

Conquer children's clothes clutter by using a rod extender to add another lower-hanging bar. Children can then hang up and take down their own clothes.

Wash stuffed toys whose tags say they're washable by putting them in a pillowcase and adding them to a wash load. Make sure to mend any small tears in them first.

Cut garden flowers early in the morning or after sundown. Take a bucket with a few inches of lukewarm water in the bottom to the garden with you. Place each stem in the bucket as you cut it. Then, when you return to the house, fill the bucket with cool water and leave the flowers in the bucket in a cool, dark place for several hours or overnight. This provides needed moisture and conditions the flowers to the indoors.

Pound the woody stems of lilacs with a hammer gently, to help them absorb water in a bouquet. Cut rose stems with a knife on a diagonal—under water if possible.

Extend the life of cut flowers by keeping them out of bright light, by changing the water every day, and by adding the following ingredients to the water:

An aspirin or 1/2 cup seltzer or carbonated water
1 teaspoon sugar

Sew on frequently popped buttons with dental floss.

Keep from snagging your panty hose by smoothing your hand with lotion before putting on the hose.

Stuff wet shoes with newspapers or paper towels to keep their shape. Let them dry away from heat.

Use a see-through travel accessory organizer to hang up your jewelry in your closet. Or store pieces of jewelry that you always wear together—like a coordinating necklace or pin and earrings—in a small zip-closure bag. Taking time to organize your accessories speeds dressing time and helps you realize and maximize your wardrobe's possibilities.

Bundle all your receipts and payment stubs by month in twelve large, heavy envelopes. In a thirteenth envelope save all Christmas gift receipts so that you can quickly place your hands on the receipt for any gift that must be returned. Each year at tax time go through your envelopes, saving what is important and tossing the rest.

Give each room a five-minute pick-up, taking an empty clothes basket and moving promptly from one room to the next. Sometimes this is enough to restore the peaceful atmosphere that clutter robs from you.

Clean the rack of a barbecue grill by using an oven cleaner or by soaking it in a solution of household ammonia and water. Scrub, rinse, and dry it thoroughly. (Be sure to wear gloves!)

Equip the room in which your overnight guests will stay with the following: an extra blanket and pillow, tissues, an empty wastebasket, and extra hangers for the closet. A small bouquet of fresh flowers lends an extra special touch.

Equip the guest bathroom with plenty of towels and washcloths, shampoo, a drinking cup for each guest, tissues, extra toilet paper, Tylenol (away from child's reach), and if possible, a hair dryer.

JUST FOR FUN

Janet wasn't tired at 11:00 P.M. when she bent to turn off the reading light and go to sleep. It was the last night of their vacation at the cabin, and she remembered something she had wanted to do.

She tiptoed into the darkness of her four-year-old daughter Karin's bedroom and sat on the edge of the bed. Gently smoothing the fine strands of tousled hair from Karin's face, Janet kissed her on the cheek and whispered in her ear. "Karin! Wake up. It's Mommy. I want to show you something special."

Janet helped a groggy Karin get dressed. As they left the cabin, Karin kept the flashlight focused on the narrow path to the lake, and clutched her mother's hand. "Mommy! What are we doing?" Karin's giggle was shivery with excitement and the cool night air.

"Shhh. We're almost there." A breeze off the water brushed their faces as they stepped out onto the wooden pier. "Karin, look!"

Along the shore a few lights winked from cabins and stores. But arching above the mountains the sky was splashed with stars like confetti, the cloudy smudge of the Milky Way through the middle.

They laid on their backs on the hard wooden slats, hands behind their heads, watching for shooting stars in a meteor shower that Janet had read was coming. As they watched patiently, a shooting star punctuated the sky like a silver dash—then vanished. They counted the shooting stars, but only the ones they both saw so neither could cheat.

"Why did God make so *many* stars, Mommy?"

And why, Janet wondered, *didn't she take time like this with Karin more often?*

———————

Laugh to release stress. When your daughter cuts her own hair two days before she's the flower girl in a wedding, or your two-year-old dumps cornstarch on the kitchen floor and swims in it, take a photo and laugh.

———————

Have a sock hop with the children. Take off your shoes and put on some of your old albums. Dance until you drop.

———————

Make bath time especially appealing after a long day. Partially fill the tub, give the children paint-brushes, and let them "paint" on paint-with-water papers you have taped to the bathtub walls.

———————

After your child's bath, dry her with a big, fluffy towel and puff on some baby powder.

Invest in perennially favorite toys. There are good reasons why they endure. A group of college students listed toys that had been their favorites: Legos, Lincoln Logs, Barbies, Strawberry Shortcake, Matchbox cars, John Deere tractors, GI Joe, My Little Pony, Tinker Toys, Silly Putty, and Play Doh.

Accumulate dress-up clothes and hats for a variety of occupations; toy workbenches, kitchens, and cash registers; and puppets, stuffed animals, dolls and doll houses for hours of childhood pretending.

Create some table talk at a family meal. Even if you are with your children several hours a day, there is a lot you don't know about them. Ask them questions such as these:
- What toy is special to you?
- Where is your favorite restaurant?
- What do you like to do with your grandparents?
- What do you remember about being a baby?
- What is your favorite book?
- What do you like to eat?
- Who is your best friend?

Invite your child to join you in an activity you enjoyed when you were young, such as hula hoop or hopscotch, climbing a tree, going fishing, or playing a favorite board game.

--- --- --- --- --- --- ---

Let your preschooler decorate her own bag to carry around her treasures. Give her a small brown paper bag or a small paper shopping bag with handles. Supply crayons, glitter glue, and plenty of stickers so she can decorate a special tote of her own.

--- --- --- --- --- --- ---

Take a special day to spend with one child doing what he likes to do.

--- --- --- --- --- --- ---

Play beauty shop. Let your child shampoo and style your hair, or paint your fingernails and toenails.

--- --- --- --- --- --- ---

Hike with your children, but don't be driven by the goal of reaching a particular destination. Most children are interested in every leaf, log, animal, or insect on the path. A favorite trail never gets boring because it changes constantly with the seasons, the weather, and the time of day. Take along a change of clothes for your children so you won't worry about dirt or mud or them wading in a shallow stream. Dress them in long pants to protect legs from insect bites, scrapes, and poison ivy, and in hats to keep off the sun or rain.

--- --- --- --- --- --- ---

Try to prevent these things, which leave a birth-day child crying: too much anticipation ahead of time, too much confusion at the party, too much attention focused on someone else, and too many children sharing the birthday child's toys. (Put away special toys ahead of time.)

———————

Use margarine tubs or baby wipe containers as molds for playing with sand or to build forts, houses, and figures in the snow. You play too!

———————

Find a big box. Do one of these four things:

- Target practice: Cut a large hole in one side of the box. With string, hang a foil pan from the top edge of the hole so the pan swings freely in the center. Throw balls at the pan.
- Castle: Construct a castle by cutting the top off the box and leaving notches along the top like on a castle wall. At the bottom, cut a door that opens down like a drawbridge.
- Puppet theater: Cut an opening in the front of the box for the theater stage and another in back for a door. Make a curtain out of an old sheet or towel to drape across the opening.
- City or airport: Cut out one side and lay the box flat to make a city or airport for toy cars or planes. Let the children help draw the roads and buildings.

———————

Take time to hold your child when he wakes up and wants to be held for a while in the morning. It helps the child to start the day well, and it helps the mom too!

Tie long strings to the necks of blown-up balloons and let children run outside with them on a windy day.

Wrap gifts with newspaper comics, fabric remnants, lunch bags, or butcher paper that your children have decorated. Add a few buttons or dried beans inside a quiet package or a rock inside a light package. Let the children help wrap the gifts.

Top a child's gift box with balloons, crayons, pencils, shoelaces, erasers, bubble pipes, hair ribbons, Matchbox cars, or party hats.

Run a pajama race when you're too tired to get the children ready for bed. The child who is ready for bed first—pajamas on, face washed, and teeth brushed—picks the story to be read. Mom or Dad can help the youngest ones if necessary. You get ready for bed too.

Bring a dishpan of snow in from outside and set it in the kitchen sink or on a towel on the kitchen floor for your child to play with.

Take a walk or bike ride with your preschooler. At each corner, stop sign, or stop light let him choose which direction to go. For more of an adventure, flip a coin at each stop to decide.

Pull out a tray—silver if you have one—and surprise your husband or your children with a breakfast or nighttime snack in bed.

— — — — — — —

Create doll clothes from outgrown infant undershirts decorated with fabric paints.

— — — — — — —

Ask your neighborhood supermarket for a behind-the-scenes tour for you and your child.

— — — — — — —

Ease young children into the camping experience with family room "camping." Drape a sheet over chairs and spread sleeping bags on the floor of your "tent." Read together by flashlight. If your child sleeps through the night, next time try the backyard before moving into the wider world.

— — — — — — —

Draw a sidewalk "track" for riding toys on the driveway.

— — — — — — —

Spark some fun at mealtime by putting a game that is age-appropriate to your child in the middle of the dinner table. Each person must take a bite before taking his or her turn.

— — — — — — —

Relax and don't sweat potty training, thumb sucking, eating peas, and the other stuff that really won't matter when your child is eighteen years old.

— — — — — — —

Ask your child for ideas for activities. He will behave better if he knows his feelings are being considered.

— — — — — — —

Divide a toddler's toys into three or four boxes and rotate a different box each week. It's like receiving new toys.

— — — — — — —

Get down on your knees and give a child a hug. Have lots of "group hugs" with the whole family.

— — — — — — —

Use your child's original artwork for gift wrap and tags, as place mats covered with contact paper, and for notecards or stationery.

— — — — — — —

Watch a rip-roaring storm together from a covered porch or patio.

PLANNING PAYS

Plumping the pillows to perfect position, Katherine lounged back in bed. A mug of coffee and two pieces of toast with currant jelly were nested among the papers and books on her bedside table. She reveled in the unaccustomed stillness of a house in which she was the only one awake. Even the dog lolled in a pool of morning sunlight.

Katherine took a small, lined yellow pad from the drawer. "Wednesday," she wrote at the top, spelling out the day with an extravagant sense of having plenty of time. "To Do." Her pen scratched tracks from one line to the next: dog for shots, groceries, call painter, pay bills. With a flourish, she stabbed ink bullets in front of each item.

The high point of the day would follow nap time. She'd roll the wading pool out of the garage so that Moselle and Alexander could splash while she washed the car. She smiled as she embellished this grand finale to an early summer's day. Maybe she'd even pull out her swimsuit ...

Sensing a presence, Katherine looked up to see three-year-old Alexander standing in the doorway. Helping him snuggle into bed beside her, Alexander looked up at her expectantly. "Mom, today let's go to Leaps & Bounds, then we'll go to the zoo, then we'll swim at the Y, then we'll have Dillon over, then we'll go get ice cream . . ."

Just as Katherine started to interject, Alexander grinned at her and concluded, "Now *that's* a plan!"

— — — — — — —

Keep on the refrigerator or wall a calendar with large daily blocks on which to record family appointments, car pools, and schedules.

— — — — — — —

Fill a "waiting bag" with paperwork, blank postcards, a tablet, a Bible, and a magazine or catalog for those times when you find yourself waiting for an appointment or to pick up children.

— — — — — — —

Keep school and activity papers together and organized with a clipboard for each child, or keep two files for each child, one labeled "School" and one labeled "Activities."

— — — — — — —

Stock up on supplies for your home desk area when school supplies are on sale. Buy bright folders to hold meeting or class notes, permanent marking pens, pencils—whatever supplies you frequently use.

— — — — — — —

Get up an hour or so before your children for some truly productive time. Take a half hour to look over the calendar and your to-do list, and organize the day. Then read the Bible, pray, reflect, and allow God to speak to you about your children and how to parent them. This time brings stability and perspective to your day.

— — — — — — —

Get ready for the day the night before. Make lunches or snacks, pack a swim bag or diaper bag, and lay out clothes and school backpacks.

— — — — — — —

Take one day at a time, and don't have too high expectations of getting a lot done. Learn to make a to-do list for the day, and then shorten it by half.

— — — — — — —

Don't be too goal-oriented. Look at things from a child's perspective, whose objective is love and fun.

— — — — — — —

Help your children with the upheaval of a move by letting them each choose two favorite toys to keep out of the packing boxes and personally carry to your new home. See that the children's beds are some of the first items situated in your new home.

— — — — — — —

Invite a new baby-sitter to come over for a snack a few days before she baby-sits. This allows you to get to know her and for her to get to know you, your expectations, and best yet, your children.

— — — — — — —

Make the best of it; forget the rest of it.

— — — — — — —

Plan an itinerary, and then cut it in half if you have young children. Instead of a five-mile hike, take a two-mile hike. Finish it off with a picnic lunch on a big rock. Instead of counting on three hours at a museum, plan on one-and-a-half, and then head for a playground or lunch.

———————

Choose your time commitments wisely. Before making a volunteer commitment, think realistically about how much time you would like to give. Give as much time and energy as you want, not as much as school groups, church groups, charities, or political groups would like you to give. When asked to volunteer, defer a decision until you stop to list all your commitments and those of other family members. Weigh your passion for another involvement against any imbalance it would cause.

———————

Develop a schedule for meals, naps, and bedtimes that is consistent enough to be healthy, but flexible enough for special times, like outings or having company. Children feel secure when routines are developed and a schedule is kept.

———————

Don't lose sight of the fact that change and variety make life interesting and fun. Hamburgers don't always have to be made with ground beef. They could be veggie burgers or salmon burgers.

———————

Encourage your children to take responsibility for dressing themselves, making their own beds, putting their clothes away, and doing designated chores. You will have more time and energy to spend with them.

Let one child stay up an hour past his bedtime once a week if you have several children and find it difficult to spend time alone with each one. If that child resists bedtime when it is not his turn to stay up, he forfeits his night with Mom and Dad's undivided attention.

Use a backpack instead of a diaper bag, to keep your hands free.

Carry individually wrapped wet wipes in your purse.

Take time while your infant is napping to "play" or do something special with your older child. Include him in what you're doing, such as baking cookies or cleaning house.

Make a list of tasks you can easily ask someone to do when they offer to help you. When you need help, ask for it. Don't assume others will somehow just know that you need it.

Label boxes of baby clothes with sizes when you pack them away so they are sorted for the next child or for giving away.

———————

Concentrate on spending time with your child after dinner. Then put him to bed early and take time for yourself.

———————

Plan a balance of indoor and outdoor activities for your children.

———————

Expect things to take more time when you are with children. If you allow extra time to find the lost shoe or Teddy bear, or for the diaper change that inevitably happens just when you're ready to leave, it will lessen your stress. If you must be somewhere at 9:00 A.M., pretend you have to be there at 8:30.

———————

If you have trouble finding a block of time to spend with your child, schedule it on your calendar. Appointments are harder to break. Let your child see Mom and Dad set dates with each other too.

———————

Put a note on the front door when Mother and Baby are resting—and remove it when they're not!

———————

Set a goal each day, such as making vacation plans, finishing a project on the computer, or sewing drapes. When the task is completed, celebrate in a way that's meaningful to you.

Style your hair and apply your makeup while your child is in the bathtub next to you so you can chat.

Keep the following lists in a small notebook in your purse:
- A running shopping list of clothes for the family and gifts and household needs so when you have the opportunity to shop and the price is right you can buy.
- Clothing sizes of family members.
- Dimensions you'll need now and then, like the length and width of your table for buying tablecloths and the size of your furnace filter.
- Gift ideas for particular people.
- A list of your family members' social security numbers.

Order from mail-order catalogs when the quality and price are right.

Let your fingers do the walking. Save time by calling ahead to see if, for example, a bookstore has a particular book in stock.

Carry colored pipe cleaners and Cheerios in zip-closure bags in your purse to occupy children in church or while you wait for appointments.

BAND-AIDS

A little after midnight, the baby's whimpering roused Dana from her sleep. By the time Dana reached her room, Sarah stood at the crib railing, crying fitfully.

Dana pulled the baby into her arms, dragging a crib blanket with her, and carried her to the rocking chair. *She feels so hot,* Dana thought, as Sarah lay limp and sweaty against her. That new fear that had come with motherhood squeezed Dana's heart. *Why did Sarah always get sick at night, when she felt so isolated from help? And why was her husband always traveling when this happened?*

With Sarah in her arms, Dana went to the bathroom medicine cabinet and peered inside. She pushed aside bottles and jars looking for the infant Tylenol. Should she take Sarah's temperature? How high was high enough for her to call the doctor? If another ear infection was coming on, should she be giving her any other medicine?

The box of brightly colored Band-Aids fell off the shelf, scattering across the counter. Not for the first time,

79

Dana wished some advice would tumble out of the box with them.

— — — — — — —

Touch test all steel decks, slides, and steps before your child gets on the play equipment. Children can suffer serious burns from metal playground equipment exposed to the sun. Very young children are most at risk because they may not react and pull away quickly enough. Explain the procedure to your child and encourage her to touch test as well.

— — — — — — —

Encourage your child to drink lots of liquids when she has a fever. Serve small amounts frequently, varying the beverage to coax her to drink. A baby bottle may sometimes be a good solution, or a snow cone of finely crushed ice with thawed frozen fruit juice concentrate poured over it.

— — — — — — —

Help a child recovering from diarrhea move from a clear liquid diet to a regular diet by serving mashed potatoes, rice cereal, Jell-O, crackers, dry toast, bananas, or applesauce.

— — — — — — —

Check with your doctor if your child runs a temperature after having a cold for a few days. She has probably developed a secondary infection such as bronchitis or an ear infection. On the other hand, a low-grade fever at the outset of a cold is usually normal.

— — — — — — —

Rub baby oil over and around bandages to help them come off more easily.

— — — — — — —

Observe three aspects of a child to determine if he is sick: appetite, appearance, and activity. If just one is out of the ordinary, the child is fine and just having an off day. If two are unusual, the child is probably sick with a minor ailment like a cold, which could be treated at home. If all three are off, the child probably needs a doctor's care.

— — — — — — —

Give your child a fruit-flavored Popsicle (still in the wrapper) instead of ice to hold on a minor bump or bruise or fat lip from a fall. Tell her that as soon as the hurt goes away, she can eat the Popsicle. It's amazing how quickly she feels better.

— — — — — — —

Try these remedies when chicken pox visits your household:
- Bathe your child in a soothing mixture of bathwater and oatmeal.
- Let your child use a small sponge shaped like an animal or object to dab anti-itch lotion onto his spots.
- Help prevent the child from scratching by putting socks or mittens on his hands, especially at night.

— — — — — — —

Adjust the crib mattress for a child who is prone to ear infections, so that the head of the crib is a notch higher than the foot. This aids postnasal drainage as the child sleeps.

— — — — — — —

Close the bathroom door and turn on the hot water in the shower full blast for a child with croup. Stay in the bathroom with the child until the croupy cough subsides.

— — — — — — —

Don't expect to get things done when your child is sick. You will be frustrated, and the child needs your comfort. Change your perspective from what you had hoped to do that day to the opportunity the illness affords for you to spend special time with your child.

— — — — — — —

Offer the mother of a newborn the gift of three free calls to you—day or night—with any type of question.

— — — — — — —

Two methods of pain-free splinter removal:
- Apply a dab of white glue over the skin where the splinter is imbedded. Let the glue dry, then peel it away. The splinter should lift out too.
- Apply a spot of liquid dishwashing soap on a Band-Aid and place the Band-Aid over the splinter overnight. The soap should draw out the splinter.

— — — — — — —

Gather these first-aid supplies for camping trips or other vacations: Band-Aids, disinfectant, antibiotic ointment, Pepto-Bismol (for S'More overdose!), acetaminophen, Benadryl, sunscreen, and an insect repellent product suitable for children.

Ways to ease your child's fears about visiting the doctor or dentist:

- Bring a stuffed animal or doll to be examined by the doctor.
- Buy a play doctor's kit and role-play at home.
- Read together picture books about a visit to the doctor before the appointment.
- Pack along a surprise for your child to play with in the examining room while you wait, such as paper and crayons or a finger puppet.

Tips for occupying a sick child:

- Place a bell or whistle by the bedside for when she really needs you.
- Give her a flashlight or magnifying glass to play with.
- Keep her company by rearranging or cleaning out her room.

HELPING
CHILDREN LEARN

Jenny and Allison were neighbors and in a baby-sitting co-op. One especially springlike afternoon when Jenny came to Allison's house to pick up her two preschoolers, the two moms sat on the front stoop and talked while the children rode Big Wheels back and forth on the sidewalk.

Jenny had four kids, the oldest two in elementary school. Allison looked up to Jenny as a wiser, more experienced parent. "What do your kids play with the most?" she asked.

"Well, lately the younger ones have played with their dolls more. Do your boys have boy dolls?" Jenny asked.

"No," replied Allison, feeling defensive. "But they've never asked for them."

"Our boys each have their own boy doll," said Jenny. "How can you expect your boys to grow up to be good daddies if they don't have dolls for practice?"

After Jenny left, Allison stewed over this. What if Jenny was right? Her boys had lots of stuffed animals, including a Snoopy and a Paddington Bear with outfits they could change, but no dolls. Tim's friend Ty across the street even had a life-sized doll which Ty's mother had made by having Ty lie on the fabric while she drew around his body. She had even given it brown hair and eyes like Ty's. Allison could never do that, but maybe she should buy a baby boy doll for her youngest son, Drew.

She sighed. How could she ever teach her children all they needed to learn?

Keep an extra chair or stool in the kitchen, in the laundry room, or in your home office so your child can easily watch what you're doing and talk to you.

Create silent family symbols, like a tug on the ear, the peace sign, or a wink and decide what they mean—"It's time to go" or "That's enough" or "You're the best!" Use them to create a sense of unity and camaraderie.

Help your child learn to distinguish shapes by pouring five or six different types of uncooked pasta in a bowl. Give your child one piece of pasta and have him feel in the bowl with his other hand to find three more of that shape of pasta.

Avoid giving children the idea that prayer time with God takes place only while they are sitting quietly at the dinner table or kneeling at their bedside. Deuteronomy 6:6–9 instructs us, as parents, to talk to our children about God at every opportunity: when sitting at home, when walking along the road, when lying down and getting up. Teach your children to praise and pray throughout the day, even as they are bouncing, hopping, skipping, and tumbling.

— — — — — — —

Try to model what your child needs to learn. Let him see in you a true reflection of living a life for Christ in an unbalanced world.

— — — — — — —

Make a ritual of walking out to the vegetable or flower garden with your child each day to investigate and discuss any changes you see. Smell the roses. Pick the beans. Pull some weeds. Plant some more seeds.

— — — — — — —

Give your child several plastic containers of different sizes, such as shampoo bottles, measuring cups, and funnels, during bath time. Pouring water from one to another increases muscle control in the hand and helps to develop hand-eye coordination.

— — — — — — —

Let your child frequently choose between two acceptable options. Either choice is a winner, and the child grows in decision-making skills.

— — — — — — —

Hand a pencil, crayon, or marker to your child toward the middle of her body. She will reach for it with her dominant hand.

— — — — — — —

Help your child learn to make choices by allowing him to choose three library books from one particular children's library shelf within a certain time limit, perhaps five or ten minutes.

———————

Teach your child where he lives by substituting his address for the words of any familiar or favorite tune. The tune "A Ticket, A Tasket, A Green and Yellow Basket" could be changed to "My name is Spencer Sumner, and this is my address . . ." In the same way teach him his phone number.

———————

Let preschoolers practice scissor skills by giving them child-safe scissors and some old magazines and catalogs and asking them to cut out pictures of eyes, noses, mouths, and hairstyles. Once they have collected a few of each, have them use a glue stick and several paper plates to make face collages.

———————

Search together for letters from your children's names when you walk or drive with them. Scan business signs and billboards, license plates and bumper stickers to find a "z" for Zack or an "m" for Amy.

———————

Take a walk with your child after a spring rain. Notice the fat worms on the cement, the fresh smell of the air, the songs of the birds.

———————

Help your child learn left from right by doing the following things:

- Ask your child to hold up both of her hands, palms facing away from her, thumbs pointing toward one another. Show her that her left index finger and thumb will always form the letter "L."
- When you wash your child's hands, say, "First, let's wash your left hand. Now we'll wash your right hand," taking each hand in turn.

Children love to hear favorite stories over and over. Tape-record your child's favorite stories, using these tips:

- Record only one story on each side of the cassette.
- Ask a neighbor or friend to record the stories for an interesting, new voice.
- Help the child match cassettes with storybooks by writing the story name on the cassette label and by affixing matching stickers on the cassette and book.
- Begin each recording by giving the title of the book, the author, and the illustrator.
- Just as on the commercial story tapes, describe the picture on the page where the child should begin, and use a bell or other noisemaker to alert the child to turn the page.
- Read with lots of expression and more slowly than you ordinarily would.
- At the end of the story, have the recording say that the child has reached the end. If he wants to listen to it again, he should press the red

(give a color) button to rewind. If all the buttons are the same color, put a colored dot sticker on the rewind button to identify it.

— — — — — — —

Get into the habit of visiting the library with your child.

— — — — — — —

Teach your children to swim as soon as they are ready. Wherever you are, swimming is usually available, and it provides hours and hours of fun. It is also an important life skill. Many gyms and community centers offer water babies swimming courses.

— — — — — — —

Keep a file of things to do, things to see, and places to go with your children.

— — — — — — —

When you are playing catch, count the tosses and catches. After your child has mastered counting up to ten, have her start counting backwards.

— — — — — — —

Teach your children that they are an important part of a family team. We each need the others to make our family unit work. Show them ways they can help. Even a two-and-a-half-year-old can make his bed and set the table, in his own way.

— — — — — — —

"Sink the battleship." Potty train a little boy by throwing a square of toilet paper into the stool and having him aim at it.

— — — — — — —

Teach children to pray by modeling prayer as a simple conversation with God.

— — — — — — —

Don't expect to cover too much ground when you take your child to a museum. Let your child lead you, and you may be surprised at what catches her attention. As you start your museum tour, discuss with your child what behavior is appropriate. Better yet, ask a guide or docent to discuss this with your child.

— — — — — — —

Put a dot with permanent marker on the inside edge of each shoe to help toddlers get shoes on the right feet. Teach them to position the shoes correctly by making the dots "kiss."

— — — — — — —

Let children speak for themselves when someone asks them a question. Don't answer for your child or correct your child's answer.

DOINGS WITH DAD

Madeline studied the bright lights of nighttime Topeka through the car window. Her father supervised a crew that repaired neon and electric signs, and one night a week she helped him check the signs for needed repairs. She took her job very seriously.

"Don't look on my side, Daddy!" she scolded, as she caught her father's gaze wander to the right side of the street.

"Okay, Maddie, I won't," he replied. He began whistling "Take Me Out to the Ball Game" and Madeline joined in, tunneling air through the hole where a front tooth had once been. Whistling was their secret. Her daddy had taught her how to whistle while they checked the signs. Most of her friends in first grade couldn't do it.

The best part of the night was just ahead. They passed her favorite sign—a giant Okay Used Cars sign with its blinking arrow of hundreds of individual lightbulbs curling around the letters. She counted the burned-out bulbs as fast as she could.

Then her dad turned down Lindenwood toward Bennie's Coffee House. The rush of aroma as her father opened the door for her made Madeline feel sixteen rather than six. They sat at a little round table on metal chairs that screeched against the cool tile floor. Madeline always had a hot chocolate with whipped cream and cinnamon—as much as she wanted—and her daddy drank his café mocha. And then they sat and talked, just the two of them, about anything and everything.

─ ─ ─ ─ ─ ─

Remember that God gave you your child's father first.

─ ─ ─ ─ ─ ─

Encourage your husband to help bathe the children and fix them meals starting when they are very young. Don't criticize him if he doesn't do things exactly as you would. Give him space to be a dad in his own way. Your children will learn there are different ways of doing things, not necessarily one right way.

─ ─ ─ ─ ─ ─

Strive for closeness with your husband by doing projects together around the house. Learn a variety of skills you can enjoy together, from sponge painting the bathroom to honing an engine block or stir frying.

─ ─ ─ ─ ─ ─

Encourage interaction between a dad and his young children by having him:

- Take the boys in the shower with him.
- Seat the child close to him so they can talk while he's shaving and dressing.
- Include the child with him on short errands.
- Hold the child, help with feedings, change diapers.
- Gently wrestle and play on the floor with the child.
- Read to the child.
- Take care of the child while Mom is away (without a long list of instructions).

Don't let the children be your world. When your husband asks you to do something or to go somewhere with him, try to make yourself available for togetherness. A strong marriage is important to your children.

Go out on a date together, once a week if possible. If the budget is tight, try to meet for lunch once a week, which is much cheaper than dinner. Talk about the children, yourselves, your dreams, your goals. Talk over the family calendar of upcoming events and about what you would like to put on the calendar together.

Encourage your husband to sometimes take your older child fishing with him or on an outing, leaving you with the youngest child to nap or relax.

Promise one another that each year you will get away for the weekend closest to your anniversary — just the two of you — and enjoy being together without schedules or children.

Encourage Dad to take one child out to breakfast each Saturday morning.

Have Dad take each child out for breakfast on his or her birthday. At breakfast, talk with each child about what goals or new things he or she would like to accomplish that year. Keep a file of these goals so that at the next birthday Dad and child can discuss them again.

Play ball! A rousing game of ball, tag, or a relay race in the backyard before dinner is a good release for Dad and the children.

Let the children wash riding toys with the hose while Dad washes the car.

Listen to what simple gesture says "I love you" to your husband. A neck rub? Shirts taken to the cleaners? Brownies in his lunch? Make the effort to say you love him in ways he will "hear."

Find ways for your husband to be involved with you and with the children. Suggest these ideas to him with the courtesy you would use when asking a friend.

— — — — — — —

Suggest that your husband select a small trinket for each of your children—something that reminds him of them—to keep in his pants pocket with his loose change. During the day, whenever he reaches for change and feels a trinket, he is reminded to pray for that child.

— — — — — — —

Set aside fifteen minutes after work for you and your husband to talk and relax together.

— — — — — — —

Remember, just as you are the mother God chose to raise your child, your husband is the person God chose to be that child's dad.

— — — — — — —

Discuss matters of childrearing and discipline when you are not with the children. Present a united front when you are with them.

— — — — — — —

Encourage your husband to establish some traditions as a dad that are all his own. One young mother tells that when she was a child her dad always baked fudge at Christmas, but wouldn't let any of the family in the kitchen lest they discover his secret recipe. Finally, when she was a teenager, she happened in on his fudge baking, only to discover he used the recipe off the jar of marshmallow creme.

— — — — — — —

Enjoy a romantic dinner for two with candle-light and music on the patio or in your bedroom when the children are in bed.

— — — — — — —

Choose a book you and your husband both enjoy, and read to each other in bed.

TIME OUT! MOM NEEDS A BREAK

Caroline entered the front door of the spa. Behind the reception desk an attractive twenty-something blond rapped her red fingernails on the appointment book. Caroline had planned to make conversation by admitting it was her first time at a spa, but now she reconsidered.

Caroline was at a resort with her husband—his company's staff conference—and the company had promised to foot the bill for one spa treatment of her choice. So she had to do something. A shampoo and hairstyle seemed safe.

Her hair did need some help. She had a bossy new permanent and was in the habit of wearing it au naturel with some gel. But the humidity at the resort had made her hair bushy and wild.

"How do you usually wear it?" Gina, the hairdresser, asked. Caroline's tongue felt thick and sluggish. How could she say, "Like this"?

"Just do whatever you want with it. Show me something new."

Gina smiled mischievously and gathered up fistfuls of frizzy hair. "Let's clip it up for volume."

After shampooing it, Gina clipped hunks of hair so that they stuck out away from Caroline's scalp. She then pulled a dryer lid over Caroline's clipped-up coiffure, cranked it to High-Hot, and disappeared. Caroline couldn't help but wonder if Gina was chortling in some closet or describing Caroline's hair to her colleagues.

When Gina returned and removed the clips, Caroline looked in the mirror in fascination. Where did she get all that hair? Gina darted the curling iron in and out to tame the curl, then teased it for yet more volume. "Now, tell me if this is too wild for you," she instructed.

"No, no. It's fine." Did she think Caroline looked like she needed to go wild?

Ten minutes later and feeling like the basket under a hot air balloon, Caroline floated out of the spa on a cloud of hair spray. So much for that adventure. Next time she would try the manicure . . . or maybe a massage.

— — — — — — —

Choose a face and body lotion that soothes the skin and has a pleasing texture and fragrance. Keep it in a pretty dispenser near the kitchen sink and in another dispenser in the master bathroom. Use it often, enjoying a moment of caring for yourself.

— — — — — — —

Wear lipstick even if you don't wear any other makeup. A moisturizer under the lipstick will help protect your lips and hold the color longer.

— — — — — — —

Take the children of a single-parent friend out birthday or Christmas shopping for her. Let them help you bake her a cake.

———————

Trade paperback books with a friend.

———————

Buy an inflatable bath pillow for a touch of simple luxury.

———————

Watch for ways you can add a touch of color or texture or fragrance to your home, maybe with potpourri, or a houseplant, or a seasonal wreath on the door. *Creating a SenseSational Home* by Terry Willits is full of great ideas.

———————

Keep a wish notebook with dividers labeled for the rooms in your home or for categories like "recipes," "arrangements and centerpieces," "holidays," and "crafts." As you see pictures in magazines and advertisements of things that appeal to you, add them to your notebook. You may find nearly as much pleasure in dreaming as you do in eventual realization.

———————

Nurture a positive attitude. Mothering is easier when you are happy with yourself.

———————

Don't try to be Supermom. Try to settle into your "new mom" role first, and as that starts to fall into place slowly resume housecleaning, cooking, and, perhaps, working.

— — — — — — —

Remember that every day is a new day. Children go through many phases, and tomorrow many things may be different.

— — — — — — —

Create your own personal oasis in your home. What is your favorite spot or room? Keep your oasis uncluttered and ready for you—even for those five- or ten-minute get-aways. In a basket keep favorite books, a Bible, magazines, or craft work. Keep an afghan nearby. Be sure the lighting is good, and keep a coaster on the table to hold a favorite beverage.

— — — — — — —

Set the atmosphere of your home with uplifting or upbeat background music rather than with TV chatter. Match the music to your moods, the weather, the time of day.

— — — — — — —

Spend time with friends who don't have children.

— — — — — — —

Enjoy what you do and always do the best you can—not the best that someone else wants or expects of you.

— — — — — — —

Sleep when your child sleeps, or do what you enjoy while your child is sleeping—whichever you need most.

Remember that "quiet times" don't have to be quiet. If you wait for quiet moments in order to pray and be refreshed by Scripture, they might never come. Your children need from you the love, strength, and wisdom only God can supply. Keep your Bible open. Pray quick, specific "arrow prayers" throughout the day. This will be a great model for your children, and someday your quiet times with God will be quiet again.

Don't feel guilty about taking care of yourself. You have to give yourself needed attention in order to be a good mom.

Catnaps can revitalize you. To help restore your energy, take a fifteen- to twenty-minute nap when the children are resting.

Constantly talk to God, the Creator, about your children. He knows them better than anyone does!

Get up and dressed even if you don't have to go anywhere the entire day.

Spend some time at the library reading a novel, listening to a best-seller on tape, or paging through a news magazine you wouldn't have time to read at home.

Take a break during the day. One home-schooling mom of four children takes a forty-five-minute rest at 1:30 P.M. each day. Each person is alone and free to quietly read, play, dream, or whatever they wish (the youngest naps). Everyone, especially Mom, comes out refreshed and ready to tackle the rest of the day.

Review the day at bedtime with an attitude of thanksgiving. This will encourage you in your mothering.

Cultivate a friendship with a woman you respect who has children a little older than yours, someone who can be a mentor to you, an encourager, if even on a casual level. It helps immeasurably to watch how such a woman interacts with her family and meets the challenges of her phase of life.

Buy yourself snow pants if you live in a cold climate so you can play outside with your children on a wintry day.

Find a good Mother's Day Out program to help you regroup, or a play group to help your child learn to play with other children.

Don't try to be a perfect mom. It only puts more stress on you, and sometimes good enough will do.

Form your own exercise co-op with other moms. Meet several times a week at the home of the one with the most exercise equipment. If none of you has special equipment, spread mats on the floor and use an exercise tape or video. Take turns watching the children or hire a sitter and split the cost.

Be observant. Savor life and learn new things each day.

Use a network of friends (like MOPS, see the page at the back of this book) to keep your sense of self.

Don't compare yourself with others. Be yourself. Be honest about your strengths and weaknesses and know that you are fully loved and pleasing to God.

Stay in touch with your friends. Develop friendships with other moms and parents with children the same age. If your husband travels frequently, find a friend who is a single parent or whose husband travels too and once a week pool your leftovers for dinner. You can talk while the children play.

Get out of the house without the children at least once a week. Hire a baby-sitter if you must. All the errands that take twice as long with the children are so much easier by yourself!

Have a teatime each day. Fix a small snack and have something hot or cold to drink. Then get away to a relaxed private place and just do nothing.

———————

Eat well.

———————

Keep a comfortable, low-maintenance wardrobe and hairstyle.

———————

Don't feel guilty when you feel you need to get away from your children. And don't hesitate to ask for baby-sitting help so that you can.

———————

Don't neglect your outside interests. Have a project or book of your own going at all times.

———————

Pray out loud when you're frustrated.

———————

Don't smother the childlike qualities inside you. They make doing things with your children much more fun. Instead of watching your child swing, swing with her. When she's catching bugs, get a container of your own and catch some too.

———————

Use fragrance strips from magazines and department store mailings as sachets for your lingerie drawers.

———————

Write a note of appreciation to your mother or an old friend. Tell her what a positive influence she has had on your life.

———————

Unclutter your bedroom. Reserve it for rest and romance.

———————

Find a partner to take a regular morning or evening walk with you. Adult conversation can make you a much better parent and a more well-rounded person.

———————

Let another pair of hands cradle your baby to give you a break.

———————

Walk outside with your newborn when nothing else seems to quiet her cries.

———————

Send the children to Grandma's for a holiday.

MOPS IS....

MOPS stands for Mothers of Preschoolers, a program designed for mothers with children under school age. These women come from different backgrounds and lifestyles, yet have similar needs and a shared desire to be the best mothers they can be.

A MOPS group provides a caring, accepting atmosphere for today's mothers of preschoolers. Here she has an opportunity to share concerns, explore areas of creativity, and hear instruction that equips her for the responsibilities of family and community. The MOPS program also includes MOPPETS, a program providing a loving, learning experience for children.

More than 2,000 MOPS groups meet in churches throughout the United States, Canada, and eleven other countries, to meet the needs of more than 70,000 women.

To find out if there is a MOPS group near you, or if you're interested in general information regarding MOPS, please write or call: MOPS International, P.O. Box 102200, Denver, CO 80250–2200. Phone: 303–733–5353 or 800–929–1287. Fax: 303–733–5770. E-mail: info@MOPS.org. Web site: http://www.mops.org.

To learn how to start a MOPS group, call 1-888-910-MOPS.

Don't miss these other great resources

NIV *Mom's Devotional Bible*

Finally, a Bible crafted just for you! The *Mom's Devotional Bible* features the complete text of the best-selling New International Version, which provides you with accuracy you can trust. And specifically for you, fifty-two weeks of Monday through Friday devotions from Elisa Morgan, president of MOPS International, are included to encourage you day by day and are filled with practical, scriptural insights. On weekends, you'll find new perspectives as you explore four "special interest" areas for moms: *A Mother's Legacy, Train Up a Child, A Time to Play,* and *Get Growing!* And from family traditions to praying for your children, twenty full-color pages add a warm, keepsake touch to the *Mom's Devotional Bible.*

Hardcover, ISBN: 0-310-92501-0
Also available in softcover and bonded leather.

**Also available from Zondervan
is a selection of
Mom's Devotional Bible
gift products.**

Mom's Devotional Bible Daybreak™
ISBN: 0-310-97055-5

Mom's Devotional Bible Journal
ISBN: 0-310-97054-7

Heartfelt Devotions for Moms
ISBN: 0-310-97052-0

Mom's Devotional Bible Gift Bag
ISBN: 0-310-97213-2

*You can find all of these great MOPS products
at your local Christian bookstore!*

ZondervanPublishingHouse
Grand Rapids, Michigan 49530
http://www.zondervan.com

from MOPS International!

What Every Mom Needs:
Meet Your Nine Basic Needs
(and Be a Better Mom)

Being the mother of a young child is a tough job, but now you can find help and understanding. In the best-selling book, *What Every Mom Needs,* Elisa Morgan and Carol Kuykendall of MOPS International point the way to relief and fulfillment in the midst of motherhood's hectic pace. After more than twenty years of research and experience with moms, MOPS has identified your nine basic needs as a mother: significance, identity, growth, intimacy, instruction, help, recreation, perspective, and hope. *What Every Mom Needs* is an invaluable resource for women who long to expand their personal horizons and become better mothers at the same time.

ISBN: 0-310-20097-0

What Every Child Needs:
Getting to the Heart of Mothering

The best-selling authors of *What Every Mom Needs,* Elisa Morgan and Carol Kuykendall, are here with a new book from MOPS to help identify what *children* really need. And not surprisingly, it is love, expressed in different ways at different times. *What Every Child Needs* points to nine basic needs, using a child's unique language of love, which helps you, as a mother, meet the needs of your child for security, play, affirmation, guidance, family, discipline, respect, independence, and hope. Each chapter will help you take an honest look at those times when your needs conflict with your ability to meet the needs of your child. As a mother, you will definitely be encouraged by this warm and inspiring book of practical thoughts and suggestions!

ISBN: 0-310-21151-4

Look for these and other MOPS products
at the Christian bookstore nearest you!

ZondervanPublishingHouse
Grand Rapids, Michigan 49530
http://www.zondervan.com

A Mother's Footprints of Faith: Stories of Hope and Encouragement

Using poignant and humorous anecdotes, Carol Kuykendall shares the value of perspective in the midst of motherhood's frantic pace. She truthfully illustrates how God often uses difficult situations to draw you closer to himself. Join Carol as she reflects on her own journey. She will help you discover wealth in the footprints leading up to where you stand now and find guidance for the rest of your journey.

ISBN: 0-310-21083-6

*Ask for these and other MOPS products
at your favorite Christian bookstore.*

ZondervanPublishingHouse
Grand Rapids, Michigan 49530
http://www.zondervan.com